ESSENTIALS

in
Ministry

BRIAN BRODERSEN

DEDICATION

To all the young men I have had the privilege of being associated with over the years, especially Michael, Char, and Braden.

CONTENTS

FOREWORD

At the dawn of the church age, the apostle Paul, inspired by the Holy Spirit, took on the task of describing and defining what the growing assembly of believers here on earth should look like. Divinely led, the apostle illustrated the church as the very body of Christ. Paul's powerful metaphor paints the picture of Jesus as the Head with believers as living, breathing tissue, bones, and organs forming an extension of the Son on earth. Believers are Jesus' body, a group of members called together to express and continue His ministry, representing His words and works to mankind.

Paul's metaphor is elaborate and well constructed. He further depicts Jesus—the Head—as desiring His body to be connected, coordinated, and cooperative with His will and wishes. We can almost picture Jesus sitting at the nerve center—the throne of God—dispatching messages to the various receptive parts of His body. He sends forth His communications to those committed to fulfilling the Great Commission, and we do our best to be the church that Jesus intended.

Today, over two thousand years have passed since Jesus entered our earthly sphere. At this juncture in human history, a lifetime of questions start and continue as we seek to discover what it looks like to be the body of Christ—the church—in the twenty-first century. Is church supposed to be a place we attend, or is it something that we are? Is it a place where we gather to face in one direction and listen to one man talk, or is it meant to be something more? What gives some churches the ability to last for generations while other churches endure for only a few years? Are we relevant enough? Are we attractive enough? The queries go on and on.

In my opinion, the most vital questions to be posed today are these: Is our contemporary expression of church recognizable as the body of Christ? Do the practices of the church resemble the ministry of Jesus? As His body, are we truly displaying Jesus or someone of our own invention?

Jesus clearly proclaimed the priorities of His public ministry from its very onset. It was on a memorable day in the synagogue in Nazareth that He picked up the scroll and quoted from Isaiah: "The Spirit of the LORD is upon Me, because He has anointed Me to preach the gospel to the poor; He has sent Me to heal the brokenhearted, to proclaim liberty to the captives and recovery of sight to the blind, to set at liberty those who are oppressed; to proclaim the acceptable year of the LORD" (Luke 4:18–19). Jesus boldly declared His job description as Messiah and then went on His way glorifying God and doing everything He said He would. As we evaluate the church all these centuries later, can people recognize the ministry of Jesus in His church?

In today's world, a few things are required of those who seek to be leaders in the body of Christ. First, a leader must be prepared to value and practice the essential lessons of ministry taught to us by Jesus Himself. Second, a leader must be willing to follow the example of the early church, who were dependent upon the Holy Spirit and heard His voice clearly and often. Finally, a leader must have integrity in his or her personal relationship with Jesus Christ. Having a vibrant and honest relationship with the Savior is the ongoing source of our power, and obedience is the basis of our ability to fulfill His mission.

In Ephesians 4, the apostle Paul wrote, "And He Himself gave some to be apostles, some prophets, some evangelists, and some pastors and teachers, for the equipping of the saints for the work of ministry, for the edifying of the body of Christ" (verses 11–12). If it is true that "He Himself" is still giving the orders and setting gifted people in place in the body of Christ, then it would benefit pastors and leaders to listen carefully to what the Head of the church has to say concerning the vital elements, expressions, and disciplines that comprise a healthy church.

Brian Brodersen does an exceptional job of bringing to light these essentials at a time when the church at large desperately needs the basics recognized and clarified once again. With candor and refreshing honesty, he challenges some of our most fundamental presuppositions about what church ought to be. *Essentials in Ministry* is brief, to the point, and filled with profound nuggets of truth for pastors, leaders, and everyday members of the church.

Tom Stipe, Senior Pastor
Crossroads Church of Denver, Colorado

PREFACE

This book was written in the context of the ministry of Calvary Chapel and for Calvary Chapel pastors. Although that is the case, my hope is that others, regardless of their affiliation, will be benefited by it. I believe that all true ministry flows from a biblical foundation and have therefore sought to lay out a biblical picture of ministry that applies across denominational lines.

Brian Brodersen
November 2007

Special thanks to Fred Field for his fellowship in the gospel.

INTRODUCTION

What are the foundational pillars upon which the church is to be built? What are the essentials of the ministry? What is the church supposed to look like today? Do we need a complete overhauling of the church to make it relevant to the mind-set of the twenty-first century? Does the Christian faith itself need to be reinterpreted or reinvented for the postmodern world? These and similar questions are being posed again and again, in book after book, by professors, pastors, ministry philosophers, cultural gurus, etc. Many of them have already decided that most pastors, and therefore, most churches, have got it all wrong and are in desperate need of a paradigm shift in their way of thinking about everything from the Bible, to the worship service, to the way Christians should live their lives in relation to the world. I couldn't disagree more with their conclusions, and I'm concerned that many of these ideas are being accepted uncritically by so many in the church today. Initially, I intended to express my disagreement in the form of a rebuttal, but I've since realized that others far more capable have already done that. Instead, I have decided simply to put forth a reminder of what ministry is all about from the biblical perspective, and to restate the essential ministry values that have been so faithfully modeled for us by Pastor Chuck Smith over the past forty years.

In my opinion, Pastor Chuck's greatest contribution to the church is that he has instilled in a new generation of men absolute confidence in the authority of the Bible and an absolute dependency on it for our understanding of the Christian life and ministry. That is our legacy, and one that we would be wise to pass on to the next generation. This book is my attempt to remind us of our heritage and to encourage us to hold fast to the things that we have received.

chapter 1

THE PREEMINENCE OF CHRIST

And He is the head of the body, the church, who is the beginning, the firstborn from the dead, that in all things He may have the preeminence.

—Colossians 1:18

The Church Belongs to Jesus

At Caesarea Philippi Peter made his great confession that Jesus is the Christ, the Son of the Living God. In verses 17–18 of Matthew chapter 16 we read, "Jesus answered and said to him, 'Blessed are you, Simon Bar-Jonah, for flesh and blood has not revealed this to you, but My Father who is in heaven. And I also say to you that you are Peter, and on this rock I will build *My* church, and the gates of Hades shall not prevail against it" (emphasis mine). Notice,

Jesus refers to the church as "My church." The first essential in ministry is to remember that the church belongs to Jesus Christ. It's not my church; it's not your church; it's not any man's church. It is the Lord's church. We are members of the body of Christ, and Jesus is the Head.[1] If we keep this at the forefront of our minds, we will do well. We will avoid many of the potential pitfalls that we all face in the ministry. We will avoid causing unnecessary pain in people's lives, and in our own lives as well. Most of the problems the church has faced over the years are the result of Jesus being replaced as the Head of the church by a man or group of men.

The first essential in ministry is to remember that the church belongs to Jesus Christ.

The moment I start to think that the church I'm overseeing is my church, or that the people I am ministering to are my people, or if I come to a place of thinking that I'm entitled to something, or I lose sight of being in the ministry by the grace of God alone,[2] that's when the trouble begins. The moment I forget that I am an unprofitable servant who's done only what is required,[3] that's when things will start to unravel! Of course, any one of us can have momentary lapses into pride and stupidity, but if we ever settle into one of these mind-sets, it won't be long before the whole thing comes crashing down on us. We are simply stewards of another man's things.[4] That man is Jesus Christ!

Led by the Lord

Since it is His church, the Lord is not expecting me to come up with a strategy to build the church; He's not looking for me to develop a five-year plan or any other corporate-driven scheme. He knows exactly what He wants to do, and all He expects of me is that I obey the instructions given in His Word and follow the leading of the Holy Spirit.

The New Testament beautifully portrays this for us, particularly the book of Acts. Here's a group of ordinary men who were called by Jesus to be the ones who would lay the foundation of His church. These men understood their inadequacies and recognized their limitations, so we see them constantly looking to the Lord for wisdom and guidance. They pray; they wait upon Him; they anticipate His direction; they look for the Spirit to lead them. In fact, all throughout the book of Acts we find statements like these: "the Spirit said"; "the Spirit forbid"; "it seemed good to the Holy Spirit," etc.[5] The apostles didn't form a planning committee and try to come up with a new strategy or some contemporary way to reach their community or relate to their culture. They didn't hire a firm to come in to do a demographic study of the area so that they could know their target group. What did they do? Acts 13 tells us: "As they ministered to the Lord and fasted, the Holy Spirit said, 'Now separate to Me Barnabas and Saul for the work to which I have called them.'" The apostolic church was under the immediate control of the Holy Spirit. Sadly, a lot of what is going on in the church today is man-driven rather than Spirit-led, but that wasn't the case with the apostles. They were utterly dependent on the leading of the Spirit.

Acts chapter 6 tells us that the apostles gave themselves continually to prayer and the ministry of the Word.[6] Notice the order: prayer first, which implies to me that they were seeking God for wisdom and direction for the ministry. There was an absolute dependency on Jesus to lead His church! Surely, these things were not written as a matter of history alone, but as a model for us to follow. If we neglect or set aside the model God has given us and try to build the church on human wisdom, we will end up building with wood, hay, and stubble; and in the end, all of our works will go up in smoke! The foundation has been laid, but let each one take heed how he builds on it.[7]

It's All About Jesus

Not only is it vital that we let Jesus lead the church, we must also give Him the place of preeminence in His church. Too many times the church becomes all about the pastor. His name is up in lights, his face is on the big screen, his voice is heard all over the campus, his word cannot be challenged, his thoughts are God's thoughts, his will is God's will.

The cult of personality dominates many fellowships today. This, I believe, grieves the Spirit and hinders the progress of the church. It interferes with the progress of the church because it places the focus on an individual, limits the ministry to that person's vision alone, and sadly but frequently channels much of the church's energy and resources toward facilitating that man and enhancing his image as a super pastor. He's got to have the best of the best as God's gifted leader: the newest car; a salary to match that of any other CEO of a large, successful corporation;

The cult of personality dominates many fellowships today.

first-class travel and hotel accommodations; tailored suits; and the list goes on.

He Must Increase, I Must Decrease

Therefore, as God's servants, we must be careful not to outshine Jesus in His church. Don't be anxious to get your name on everything. Share the ministry with others. It can too easily become a "one-man show." Don't build everything around yourself. Realize that God has gifted others, and don't be afraid to let them share the ministry with you. Remember the church at Antioch?[8] There were prophets and teachers … Barnabas, Simeon, Lucius, Manaen, and Saul. How about the team of Paul, Silvanus, and Timothy? The New Testament picture of ministry is that of a team. Some pastors, just like some athletes, are not team players. They often see themselves as owner, manager, and star player all wrapped into one. In the long run, this will prove detrimental to the ministry.

The church was not built on Peter, Paul, James, or John, but on the foundation of the apostles (plural) and prophets (plural), Jesus Christ being the chief cornerstone![9]

Remember, it's not about you or me; it's about Jesus Christ. He must increase; I must decrease![10]

chapter 2

THE WORD IN PROPHETIC POWER

*For our gospel did not come to you in word only,
but also in power, and in the Holy Spirit.*

—1 Thessalonians 1:5

The Priority of Teaching the Word

Most people who are even remotely familiar with
Calvary Chapel would more than likely identify us
as a Bible-teaching ministry. That is accurate. Bible
exposition is one of the hallmarks of the ministry
of Calvary Chapel. Sadly, this is not the case with
much of the church today. In fact, some churches actually scoff at the idea. They couldn't imagine doing
something as old-fashioned and outdated as teaching the Bible. I've witnessed this attitude firsthand.
A friend, who is a vicar in the church of England,

once estimated that out of approximately three hundred churches in a particular diocese, perhaps only twenty of those churches were led by men who believe the Bible to be the Word of God. That's tragic! Unfortunately, even many who claim to believe the Bible to be the Word of God wouldn't necessarily see the exposition of the Scriptures as a priority for the church today. This is undoubtedly one of the main reasons for the current irrelevance of the church and its declining influence upon the culture.

Preach and teach the Word—the very life of the church depends on it!

It is because Christian people are not being taught the Word that they are not able to be the light of the world and the salt of the earth; and subsequently the church is being trampled under the foot of men. When I see churches being converted into performing arts centers, restaurants, a block of flats, or even into mosques, I think of the solemn words of Jesus, "If the salt loses its flavor … it is … good for nothing."[11] Preach and teach the Word—the very life of the church depends on it! It has the power to save lives, change lives, and give life.

Study to Show Yourself Approved

Since God has called us to be teachers of the Word, we've got to be students of the Word. Study your Bibles. Get to know your Bible above and beyond everything else. Go through it meticulously. Read it, meditate on it, study it, and memorize it. This is our calling.

Today, we have so many great tools to help us study the Bible. We have written commentaries, audio commentaries, online study helps, etc. Tap into these resources and go through the Bible with a gifted Bible teacher. Make it a discipline in your life. Damian Kyle[12] once said that he went through the Bible with Pastor Chuck several times while working as a lineman for the phone company. That was his training for the teaching ministry to which God would later call him. And what a powerful teaching ministry he now has!

The primary responsibility of the pastor is to teach God's Word to God's people. So as Paul said to Timothy, "Study to show yourself approved to God," and "Preach the Word"![13]

The Word and the Spirit

Having said all of that, there is another critical

11

aspect to the ministry of the Word. Some overlook this spiritual dimension, but in my opinion, it is the very essence of teaching the Word. I'm referring to the prophetic element. I believe the teaching ministry modeled by Pastor Chuck is unique in many ways, not merely because he deliberately goes through the entire Bible verse by verse, chapter by chapter, book by book, but because as he teaches, there is a dependency on the Holy Spirit to illuminate and apply the Word to the lives of the hearers. The study of the Bible is not seen as an end in itself, but as a means to the greater end of loving, worshipping, and serving God. This is what happens when the Spirit brings to life the Word to the hearts of His people. This is why we must always maintain a dependence on the Holy Spirit as we teach the Word.[14]

The church is supposed to be a place where people sense God's presence and hear His voice.

Have you ever gone to church or sat and listened to a sermon or Bible study where all the right things were said and the facts were accurate, but the message just didn't seem to have any real power? It was perhaps good information, but there was no prophetic element. There was no dynamic sense of God speaking through the preacher. The church is supposed to be a place where people sense God's presence and hear His voice. The preacher's voice should be the medium through which the Lord can speak to His people.

Because of this we need to do our best in preparing not just our heads, but our hearts as well so there is a sensitivity to the Holy Spirit and an openness to be led by the Spirit as we teach and preach the Word. This openness to the Spirit, I believe, best explains what has happened with the ministry of Calvary Chapel. God has taken ordinary men, filled them with His Spirit, and put His Word in their mouths. The thing that I'm concerned about is that we don't lose sight of that fact and start to think that it is somehow related to our own brilliance or charisma.

My friend Bil Gallatin[15] related a story that illustrates my point. One day, he went completely blank in the pulpit and many in his church thought that he had had a stroke. As he made his way back to his office, the Lord spoke to him that this was just a reminder of where his ability to teach came from! We all need to remember that! When we begin to think that we've mastered the art of preaching or that we are now experts in sermon preparation and delivery, that's the moment the power goes out of our preaching! Although one might possess a great intellect and powers of speech and therefore be able to impress the minds of men, that kind of preaching cannot penetrate the heart. For over thirty years, God has been speaking directly into the lives of men and women through the various Calvary Chapel pastors. The common responses of people sitting in churches throughout the movement testify to that.

God has taken ordinary men, filled them with His Spirit, and put His words in their mouths.

Frequently, I hear comments like these: *As I sat in church and listened to the message, I felt like I was the only one there, and God was speaking directly to me; I came in today with a head full of questions and you answered every one of them; Someone must have told you I was coming because you were talking about me; I've been struggling with certain things in the Bible, and you cleared up all my confusion.* I have had these kinds of things said to me literally hundreds of times over the years of pastoral ministry. What is the explanation? (It certainly isn't because I'm such a gifted orator that I overwhelm people with my brilliance and charm.) It is the Word ministered in prophetic power! That's what God intends the ministry of the Word to be—not an exercise of human wisdom and ability, but a demonstration of the Spirit's power.

I'm sure this is what Paul meant when he said to the Thessalonians, "Our gospel did not come to you in word only, but also in power, and in the Holy Spirit."[16] Every preacher and teacher of the Word should aspire to this basic standard. And this, I believe, is what the Scriptures refer to when they state that God gives to the church apostles, prophets, evangelists, and teachers.[17]

Equipped to Teach the Word

In relation to the ministry of the Word, there's one other area that I feel compelled to touch on. We've already looked at the importance of study and preparation, but some might be wondering about the place of seminary or a "formal education."

As the ministry of Calvary Chapel expands around the world, that question becomes more relevant because in many countries the idea that you could teach the Bible or effectively pastor a church without a seminary degree is completely foreign. Let me answer this question by telling my story.

A Personal Testimony

A few years ago, after more than twenty years of pastoral ministry, I decided to enroll in seminary. My reasons were as follows: One, I wanted to have a little more structure and discipline at this particular stage of my life. Two, I felt a degree might be helpful in opening more doors for ministry, especially abroad.

As I began the courses, I really enjoyed them but I soon found that my busy schedule was not conducive to the study demands. Before too long, I began to get frustrated because I had already paid for the entire program and was realizing that it was going to be extremely difficult to complete it. Then one day, as I was considering the whole matter, the Lord spoke to me and said, "I didn't lead you to enroll in seminary, and I don't want you to get a degree." I immediately recognized my mistake and dropped out of the program.

Please don't misunderstand me. I'm not putting down the value of education or saying that no one should ever under any circumstances go to seminary. Each person must make his own decision. I'm merely relating my experience and how the Lord has led me. God has not called me to a get a seminary education.

I have many friends who have gone to seminary; in fact, I recently wrote a letter of recommendation for a friend of mine to be accepted into a doctoral program. My point is this: if we make formal education a prerequisite for ministry, we make a big mistake because there is no such requirement found anywhere in Scripture; and by imposing this standard, we could possibly keep many anointed men from fulfilling God's true calling upon their lives.

From a practical standpoint, I would have been really discouraged in my attempts to serve the Lord had I thought a seminary education was necessary for getting into the ministry. My background was completely devoid of any academic emphasis. I came straight out of the surf culture into the church. Getting an education was the last thing on my mind in those days. I spent my high school days ditching class and surfing rather than studying. When I became a Christian, I could barely comprehend anything I read, and my vocabulary was based primarily on the television shows I watched and the music I listened to. That's the reality. I had no interest in academics whatsoever.

Looking back, it was a very shortsighted and ignorant way to go about life, but that's where I was at nonetheless. With that background, you can perhaps imagine my experience when I first attempted to read the King James Bible. I thought that it was written in a foreign language! I didn't know twentieth century English, let alone a language from four hundred years ago.

I'll never forget when I first met my wife, Cheryl. She was a university student and an English major at that. When she suggested that we read our Bibles together, I just about died. Reading to myself was hard enough; reading out loud in front of another person was out of the question! She persuaded me that we ought to read together because that's what good Christian couples do. I'll never forget the feeling I had when she read that first chapter. It was a feeling of both amazement and terror. I was amazed at her brilliance and ability to articulate. I was in terror because I was going to have to read the next chapter. When my turn came to read, you would have thought I was an elementary school student rather than a twenty-three-year-old man. I didn't know the pronunciation or the meaning of probably a quarter of the words I read. I felt like an absolute idiot. That was my background and yet God called me to teach His Word.

I trust you have gathered by now that I can read

a bit better today. I can even spell. But all joking aside, I honestly attribute my personal growth to the work of the Spirit in my life, and that to me is the essence of Calvary Chapel, what it is really all about. I can think of many who have traveled similar paths who have become integral parts of the ministry. I think of men like Nick Long, who is the pastor of Calvary Chapel Siegen, Germany.[18] Nick was so brain dead as a result of drug and alcohol abuse that he didn't think he'd ever recover from that state. After coming to Christ, he sensed God's healing touch upon his mind. One night during a worship service, the congregation broke out in praise, singing the chorus "Our God reigns." Nick, not knowing the words, thought they were singing "I've got brains" and heartily joined in. It made perfect sense to him because that accurately described his experience.

God Wants to Use You

To me, the great distinctive of Calvary Chapel is that it is a God-made ministry. We are people who have been touched by God, and the explanation for the work He's doing through this ministry is not in us, but in Him. I'm not saying that unless you were mentally burnt-out or illiterate at one time, you can't be used by God. What I am saying is that even if you were, God can and will still use you. How? He'll renew your mind and teach you the knowledge of His Word by His Spirit. That's the testimony of many pastors in the Calvary Chapel movement: Jeff Johnson, Pancho Juarez, and Steve Mays, just to name a few.[19]

chapter 3

THE BEAUTY OF SIMPLICITY

*For our boasting is this: the testimony of our
conscience that we conducted ourselves in the
world in simplicity and godly sincerity, not with
fleshly wisdom but by the grace of God, and
more abundantly toward you.*

—2 Corinthians 1:12

Keep it Simple

Another key element in the ministry of Calvary
Chapel is simplicity. Complexity gradually occurs
in almost every human endeavor. Just look at any
human government and you will see what I mean.
Simplicity in ministry is not merely a personal
preference. It is a God-ordained mandate for the
church.[20]

The more the Spirit of God is in control of a ministry, the simpler it will be. I read a book on ministry philosophy that was so complicated, I was exhausted by the time I finished it. My thought at the end of the book was if I had to do ministry like that, I'd quit! Thank God He's made it simple. I don't have the energy required to follow all the steps to build a "successful" church laid down by hyperactive church-growth gurus. I'm so glad we can depend on Jesus to build His church! I don't have to worry about every possible problem, anticipate every single mistake that I might make, or live in fear that I might fail. My goal is obedience, and I have the Holy Spirit to teach and guide me.

Simplicity in ministry is not merely a personal preference. It is a God-ordained mandate for the church.

An acquaintance of mine recently told me about a church he visited. The Sunday morning service was a major production that went something like this: The pastor began his "talk," and after a few minutes, he directed the people's attention to a large screen where a film clip from a popular movie illustrated his point. After the film clip, he continued his talk and then went on to illustrate his next points by having the band play a song and the drama team do a skit. The service was more like a Broadway production than anything resembling the church as pictured in the pages of Scripture.

This model of ministry is dependent on all the wrong things, and it is the antithesis of what the New Testament church was doing. I'm of the persuasion that if you can't do church with just a Bible and singing a cappella or perhaps with the accompaniment of an acoustic guitar, then you've lost sight of the simplicity seen in the New Testament. This is not to say that you can only do church with a Bible and an acoustic guitar, but if you think you need anything more than that, you've lost sight of the New Testament picture. The early believers were brought together by their love for one another, their common experience of an intimate relationship with the Living God, and their thirst to learn about Jesus— the Word of God—not to participate in the latest technological advances or to be entertained by some professional road show.[21]

Am I suggesting that we shouldn't use current technology? Not at all. The danger is not in utilizing technology, but in abusing it. The simplicity of the gospel can get lost in the din and the clamor of media and images, which seems to be what is happening with some ministries today. Don't build your ministry around these kinds of things, where the medium becomes the message. Having state-of-the-art equipment or the ultimate worship band is not the goal. These things can be a blessing to clarify or frame the message if kept in the proper perspective, but they can also become a curse and a distraction when overemphasized.

Saul's Armor

The essence of what we are doing is to be simple. I think people are looking for simplicity and appreciate it when they see it. It has an authenticity about it and being authentic is good. A great illustration of simplicity is seen in the story of David battling Goliath. When David volunteered to fight Goliath, Saul suggested that David wear his armor. At the time, David was probably in his mid-teens and of just average size; Saul was a grown man who stood head and shoulders above all in Israel.[22] As David attempted to utilize the armor, he realized immediately that it would never work. The armor evidently overwhelmed David, and so he declined to use it. David opted for a much simpler weapon—a sling! I can picture in my mind's eye Goliath all decked out in what appeared to be impenetrable armor, standing ominously before the camp of Israel threatening, blaspheming, and cursing. David faces off with the giant with only a sling and a stone. Oh, the beauty of simplicity! That's God's way of doing things.

As the church adopts the methods of the world—contemporary culture and all of its entrapments—and takes on all the complexity and confusion of human wisdom, I can't help but feel that there is a parallel to Saul's armor. The church is trying to attract the world by utilizing its techniques. This is not God's way, and in the end, it's doomed to fail. I say that because once you start down that road, it's difficult to turn back. There seems to be an insatiable appetite for things bigger, better, and newer. Keep it simple. Follow the example of the apostle Paul, who conducted his ministry in simplicity and godly sincerity,[23] rather than some church-growth expert who will only turn your ministry into a bureaucratic nightmare and maybe even send you to a rest home for burned-out pastors!

> *The church is trying to attract the world by utilizing its techniques.*

chapter 4

FILLED WITH THE SPIRIT

But the manifestation of the Spirit is given to each one for the profit of all.

—1 Corinthians 12:7

Baptized in the Spirit

The baptism with the Spirit was not optional for the apostles nor should it be for us. Jesus had commissioned them to go into all the world with the gospel, but commanded them to wait in Jerusalem until they were endued with power from heaven.[24] Jesus saw this as absolutely essential to fulfilling their calling. And I believe it is essential for us in the twenty-first century as well. The Lord wants to empower us for ministry. Remember, it's "'Not by might nor by power, but by My Spirit,' says the LORD of hosts."[25]

27

God has supplied us with power. We would be fools to think that we could do this job without total dependency upon that power.

How does that power become a reality in our lives? It happens as we acknowledge our need and ask the Lord to empower us.

I pray for a fresh empowering of the Spirit regularly. I don't trust in what happened twenty-five years ago, ten years ago, three years ago, or even three months ago. I need to be continually filled with the Spirit! How does that occur? By simply asking. Jesus said, ask and you shall receive. He then said, "If you then, being evil, know how to give good gifts to your children, how much more will your heavenly Father give the Holy Spirit to those who ask Him?"[26]

The Lord wants to empower us for ministry.

Body Ministry

The question might arise—are the gifts of the Spirit for the church today? I see no reason whatsoever to believe otherwise. I don't think the church can properly function or accomplish its God-given tasks without the gifts of the Spirit. Every member of Christ's body needs to be baptized with the Spirit and using the gifts that God has given them. In order for this to happen, we need to encourage the use of the gifts and give people the opportunity to exercise them.

We read that the first church continued steadfastly in the apostles' doctrine and in fellowship.[27] Fellowship was a key component in the church. The Greek word for "fellowship" is *koinonia*, which can be translated as communion, communication, contribution, or distribution. This one word gives a picture of what was going on in the first church in Jerusalem. The people were communicating their gifts to one another, each person was contributing, and the Spirit was distributing the gifts for the building up of the body. Many of our services today center around the gifts of just a few people, mainly the pastor and the worship leader; the rest of the congregation rarely have the opportunity to share their gifts with each other. I believe it's the responsibility of the pastors to lead the people to minister to one another in this area. This is something the Lord has been putting on my heart for quite some time.

A few years ago, I began to notice that everything about our meetings was so completely predictable: open in prayer, twenty minutes of singing, forty-five minutes of Bible study, close in prayer, the end.

I began to ask myself, where is the body ministry? Some would say that that's what happens after the service. But with today's busy schedules, that might be wishful thinking. Let's be honest, most people are out the door and in their car five minutes after the service has ended. There are the faithful few who stick around afterward, but much of that time is spent just catching up with friends or maybe a little bit of prayer and further sharing of the Word. However, the picture Paul describes of the body ministering to itself in love seems to be conspicuously absent.[28] Seeing this led to the conviction that we needed to adjust the way we did things.

After praying about all of this, the Lord clearly led me to change the structure of our Saturday evening service. We still open with prayer and worship and then get into the study of the Scriptures, but rather than ending with that, we have added a time of worship and body ministry at the end of the service. After the study time, I often share briefly on the need for the baptism of the Spirit and then give opportunity for those who would like to receive the baptism to be prayed for. If people are sick or suffering, I have them stand, encouraging those nearby to lay hands on them and pray for them. I also encourage those praying that if they have a word from the Lord for that person, they should then share it with them during the time of prayer. Sometimes I'll explain the gifts of prophecy, word of wisdom, and word of knowledge, and then we'll wait to see if the Lord would want to minister to us through those gifts. Occasionally, we'll just spend time praising and thanking the Lord, and perhaps someone will have an utterance in tongues that will be interpreted. I believe this experiential element is missing from many of our churches.

Experiencing God

Have you noticed that the younger generations are hungering for an experience with God, and many of them are leaving Bible-based churches for more experience-oriented gatherings? We must remember that our churches need to be places where people not only learn about God but also experience Him. In 1 Corinthians 12, Paul refers to the manifestation of the Spirit. *Give place for fellowship in the truest sense of the word.* What does that mean? It means that God is manifest among His people, as the body ministers to itself in love through the gifts. As Paul said regarding prophecy, if one who is ignorant or unlearned comes among you and someone prophesies, he will fall on his face, the secrets of his heart will be revealed, and he will confess that God is truly among you.[29] That's experiencing God! Covet earnestly the best gifts.[30] Give place for fellowship in the truest sense of the word.

chapter 5

THE SUPREMACY OF LOVE

Now the purpose of the commandment is love from a pure heart, from a good conscience, and from sincere faith.

—1 Timothy 1:5

The Second Greatest Commandment

The final essential component in ministry is love. Both Jesus and the apostles made it clear that love is supreme. Jesus said His disciples would be identifiable by their love for one another.[31] Paul said the purpose of the commandment is love from a pure heart.[32] Peter said to love one another fervently with a pure heart; and John said he who does not love does not know God, for God is love.[33] The witness of the church has been marred many times over by our failure to love one another, and more often than not, the divisions and factions that have arisen and caused so much harm have been over petty, non-essential issues. We so easily become critical of our brothers, competitive, and envious of others. We get upset if someone moves into what we perceive to be our territory. The history of the church is filled with sad and tragic examples of Christians fighting against each other, sometimes even literally!

The witness of the church has been marred many times over by our failure to love one another.

We, as a movement, have had our own share of "church wars," "pastor wars," "theological and philosophical wars," etc. I've even seen a few cases where it's almost become physical! As men who are part of a fellowship of churches, we need to remember that loving each other is one of the main things that Jesus said would mark us as His disciples. We might not always agree with everything someone else is doing, but true Christian love will look past those differences, believing the best, and endeavoring to maintain the unity of the Spirit in the bond of peace.[34] As Peter exhorted, have *fervent* love among yourselves, for love *covers* a multitude of sins.[35] If love can cover a multitude of sins, it certainly should cover our disagreements!

Disagreeing Agreeably

I am convinced that the Lord is calling us back to this fundamental truth of the supremacy of love—among ourselves and beyond ourselves to the larger body of Christ. I might not agree with a particular philosophy of ministry, but do I have the right to speak out uncharitably against those with a different ministry philosophy? I don't agree with certain theological perspectives, but would I deny that there are many godly men and women who hold different theological perspectives from mine? We need to be full of grace and love for all of God's people. He loves them, and we obviously should too. I'm not saying that we shouldn't address, discuss, or even debate some of the issues that might concern us, but we need to do so from a heart of love, a desire for unity, and with the recognition that these are God's people and our brothers and sisters in Christ.

Over the past few years, two things have increased my awareness that the body of Christ stretches far beyond the boundaries of our own movement. The first has been my experience in ministry internationally, especially in Britain. When we moved to London to start a church, we were the only Calvary Chapel in a city of some nine million people. We learned very quickly to appreciate the larger body of Christ. It also became evident to me that if we insisted on some "exclusive" position for Calvary Chapel within the body of Christ, our ministry would have been shot down before it ever got off of the ground. Over the years, we have learned to embrace and appreciate those who are in some cases doctrinally and philosophically on a completely different page than we are. On many occasions, I have found myself fellowshipping with and being blessed by those who hold different views than I do on everything from eschatology to the ministry of the Spirit, not to mention the philosophical differences regarding ministry style.

We need to be full of grace and love for all of God's people.

Our ministry in the UK has partnered us with believers from many different church backgrounds: Anglicans, Baptists, Methodists, and Pentecostals, just to name a few. It has been a blessed experience indeed. Please don't misunderstand me. I'm not talking about joining hands with those who have denied the faith, or trying to establish some kind of unity at the expense of truth. I'm referring to those true believers who have committed their lives to Jesus and to His Word, and yet may hold different views on non-essential doctrines. We want to avoid majoring in the minors, so to speak. We can certainly hold to our convictions, but we must avoid the tendency toward animosity and division (so prevalent in our fallen nature) and learn to disagree agreeably.

The Church Is Bigger Than You Think

The second thing that has given me a broader view of the body of Christ is my experience on the live radio program, "Pastors' Perspective." Several times a week, I talk with people from a variety of different church and denominational backgrounds. It's been a real blessing and privilege to speak with Lutherans, Presbyterians, Baptists, Pentecostals, and even Catholic and Orthodox believers. I have had many lengthy discussions with those of different theological persuasions and have come away blessed to see God's work in places that I wouldn't have necessarily expected to see it. As someone has said, "The church is bigger than you think." It's clear from Scripture that Jesus Christ intends something more for His church than we've perhaps realized—something that goes far beyond the borders of a church, movement, or denomination—and encompasses people from all around the world. The Scriptures refer to the church as a nation—a nation in which men and women love each other.[36] Isn't that a beautiful picture? People loving each other; people helping each other; people encouraging each other; people building one another up; people looking out for their neighbor; people putting the needs of others before themselves; people from every tribe, tongue, and ethnic group. That's the picture of what the church is to be. The church is to be marked first and foremost by love—love for God, love for one another, and love for those who have yet to come to know Christ. Our churches should be places where people can come and find love in the truest sense. As people look at the church today, is that what they see? Or do they perhaps see a church that is bitter, angry, condemning, and loveless?

Love Never Fails

When the love of Christ is no longer the driving force of a ministry, the church loses its uniqueness, beauty, and ultimately, its attraction. When love is gone, power so often takes its place; and historically, when that has happened, the church has become an oppressor rather than a liberator; Christians have become "crusaders" rather than missionaries; and sinners have become enemies to be vanquished or foes to be conquered rather than precious souls to be saved! Paul said, "Love does its neighbor no harm."[37] Oh, the harm that could have been averted had the church remembered to love. We cannot undo the past, but by the grace of God, as we walk in love, as Christ loved us, we can certainly avoid repeating it. The Holy Spirit's word in 1 Corinthians says it all:

> *Though I speak with the tongues of men and of angels, but have not love, I have become sounding brass or a clanging cymbal. And though I have the gift of prophecy, and understand all mysteries and all knowledge, and though I have all faith, so that I could remove mountains, but have not love, I am nothing. And though I bestow all my goods to feed the poor, and though I give my body to be burned, but have not love, it profits me nothing. Love suffers long and is kind; love does not envy; love does not parade itself, is not puffed up; does not behave rudely, does not seek its own, is not provoked, thinks no evil; does not rejoice in iniquity, but rejoices in the truth; bears all things, believes all things, hopes all things, endures all things. Love never fails. ... And now abide faith, hope, love, these three; but the greatest of these is love.*[38]

LAST WORDS

My prayer is that this book has been an encouragement to you. Undoubtedly, many more subjects could have been addressed, but to me these are the foundational pillars that we must continue to build on as long as the Lord may tarry. Many of us know these things and take them for granted, but as the ministry of Calvary Chapel spreads around the world, others are looking for clear biblical directives and a model to follow as they seek to build the church in their countries. I hope in some small way that this book has helped to fulfill that need.

appendix

PRAYER

Then He spoke a parable to them, that men always ought to pray and not lose heart.

—Luke 18:1

The gospel of Luke emphasizes more than any other gospel the humanity of Jesus Christ. And in emphasizing the humanity of Jesus, Luke tells us more about the prayer life of Jesus than any other gospel writer.

Let's look together through Luke's eyes at Jesus in prayer and see what lessons there are for us.

I want to begin with two quotes, one from E. M. Bounds and the other from Samuel Chadwick. These were written in the late 1800s and early 1900s respectively, yet they are completely applicable to our current situation: "What the Church needs to-day is not more machinery or better, not new organizations or more and novel methods, but men whom the Holy Ghost can use—men of prayer, men mighty in prayer. The Holy Ghost does not flow through methods, but through men. He does not come on machinery, but on men. He does not anoint plans, but men—men of prayer."[39] "Prayer is more important than organization, more powerful than armies, more influential than wealth, and mightier than all learning. Prevailing prayer makes men invincible."[40]

I love these quotes. They remind us of how vitally important prayer is to our own lives personally. But they also apply to the church itself, specifically in the context of the ministry.

As we look at Luke's gospel, beginning in chapter 5, verse 16, we read, "So He Himself often withdrew into the wilderness and prayed." Two things stand out to me. First, Jesus *withdrew* to pray. Now, we all know that we can pray any time, any place, and that's one of the wonderful blessings of prayer. I can pray lying down on my bed, driving down the road in my car, or walking from place to place on the jobsite or through my neighborhood. However, it's very important that we take time to get away from all of the craziness of our lives and get alone with the

Lord. That's what Jesus did; He withdrew. He got away from the crowds. He got away from the people. He got away from all of the activity and spent time alone with His Father. We need to follow His example.

Consider this: If Jesus, the Son of God, sensed a need to get alone with His Father, how much more do we need to get alone with God? We desperately need to have those times of intimacy with the Lord. I think that we are probably living in the busiest time in history. There are more distractions, more things vying for our attention and our time than ever before in the history of the world. Technology has advanced; and behind that was the desire, to some extent, to free up our time. But yet, in some ways it seems to have backfired. I'm very thankful for the mobile phone, but I get far more calls now than I used to get. Something that originally was a convenience has now enslaved me. If I go out of the house in the morning and don't have my phone with me, I feel like I'm naked. All of a sudden, I'll go into a panic. And the worst thing is sometimes I'll go into a panic looking for my phone, and I'm actually talking on it. Now, that's pretty scary.

Then there's computers, the Internet, and email. Before the advent of email, I might have written a maximum of twenty letters a year. Now I have to write twenty letters a day. Don't get me wrong, I thank God for email; it's an amazing tool. Yet, it's brought so much more activity into my already busy life that I didn't really need. Because of all of this busyness, we have to give an extra effort these days to just spend some quiet time with the Lord. That's what Jesus did, and we must as well.

The second point is He withdrew *often*. He did it frequently. And the more often we get away with the Lord, the better off we're going to be, the better off things around us are going to be, and ultimately, the better off the world that we live in is going to be. Sometimes people think foolishly, "Oh, I don't have time to pray. I've got so many other things that I've got to do." If we're too busy to pray, we have a complete misunderstanding of the way the Christian life ought to be lived.

My experience has been that when I take the time out and step away from all of the busyness to spend time in prayer, I become much more effective in what I'm doing. I often realize that a lot of things that I think I have to do aren't necessary. I'm able to give over to God the unnecessary burdens that I've been carrying, which frees me to zero in on those particular things that I do have to deal with. And through prayer and spending time with the Lord, I'm given the grace and strength needed to do it. And so Jesus set us this example. He withdrew, and He withdrew often to pray.

In Luke chapter 9, verse 18, we have another picture of Jesus in prayer: "And it happened, as He was alone praying, that His disciples joined Him." Now, I want to be a person who can influence others for Jesus Christ. I want people to join me in walking with and following the Lord. But my question is: How can I become a man of influence and have that power of attraction so that people will be drawn to the Lord through me? Well, I think we see the answer here. Jesus is alone praying, and His disciples come to Him.

Here's what happens. When we get alone and spend time with the Lord, we actually become more like Him. And as we grow more into His likeness, the more attractive we become to people. I think Jesus was the most attractive person who ever lived. He wasn't necessarily attractive in the physical sense. Isaiah seems to indicate that there was nothing extraordinary about His physical form.[41] But yet, Jesus had this incredible power to attract people. He was a people magnet, and He drew the masses to Himself. Is it possible that we too could have people drawn to us that they in turn might be drawn to the Lord through us? I think the possibility increases as we spend time with the Lord, because it's there that we become more and more like Him.

People often ask, "Why do we pray?" The reasoning behind that question goes something like this: "If God is who you say He is, if He knows everything, doesn't need my help, and will get everything done that He intends, then why do we pray in the first place?" Many have asked that question, and it's valid. Why do we pray? There are at least three reasons. First and simply, God has told us to pray. We must accept that God doesn't always explain certain things. He just says, "I want you to do this," and because He's God, we need to respond in obedience. Second, we pray because God wants us to partner with Him in the work that He's doing. God has invited us to be co-workers with Him. That's an amazing thing. God doesn't *need* us; quite honestly, we don't bring a whole lot to the table. In fact, I don't bring anything that God needs.

It's sort of like the experience I had with my younger son, Braden. I remember when he was small, I had to do some plumbing work at home. There I was cramped under the bathroom sink. It was a tighter spot than I could even fit in, and there I was in all of my frustration, all twisted up under the sink trying my best to get this leak stopped. Next thing I know, my little boy, with plastic tool kit in hand, is climbing into the cupboard and trying to arrange himself on my chest so he can help me fix the thing. Now, needless to say, that didn't really help the plumbing problem. It was a precious moment, for sure. It's a moment that I cherish in my memory. But it didn't help me solve the problem. It created a bigger problem than actually fixing the one that existed. And that's similar to the way it is with God. God doesn't need us to do anything, but He actually wants us to participate with Him. And the amazing thing is that in the end, He's going to reward us for having participated with Him, even though we didn't do a whole lot.

The third, and in my opinion, the main reason we are to pray is because prayer benefits us. God wants us to pray because He knows that we need to come into His presence as often as we possibly can. When we're in His presence, He is able to do the work in our lives that needs to be done. Therefore, God bids us to come and pray so that He might transform us into His image. Our alone time with the Lord is reminiscent of Moses, who went up on the mountain and spent forty days and nights with the Lord. Remember what happened? The very image of God was impressed on Moses, so that when he came down the mountain, his face shone with such glory that the children of Israel couldn't bear to look at him.[42] And Paul tells us, "If the glory of the old covenant was such, how much greater is the glory of the new covenant?"[43] In other words, if Moses came down the mountain shining, how much more should we be shining when we come out of our prayer closet having spent time looking into the face of Jesus Christ? That's why we pray, and that's what we're talking about here. Jesus set the example. He got alone with God, and His disciples were drawn to Him. As we get alone with the Lord, we will become people of influence as well.

In verse 29 of Luke 9, Jesus is on the Mount of Transfiguration with Peter, James, and John: "As He prayed, the appearance of His face was *altered*." Jesus was transfigured, and the glory resident within Him broke forth from behind the veil of His humanity. Notice when this took place: "As He prayed ..." The word altered means changed. Prayer changes things! We live in a world that desperately needs change. We live in a world that needs to be radically altered. And we don't have to look to places like Iraq or to North Korea to see the need for change. We can just look, quite often, right into our own hearts, our own families, our own homes, our own communities, and even our own churches. We can look all around us and see the need for serious alteration. How is change going to come? Change comes through many different means, but the greatest changes come through prayer.

In prayer, we have access to the throne of heaven. We have access to Almighty God. But how many times have we thought in our frustration about a problem and wished we could to talk to someone in charge! The state of California has many problems, so why don't we all just go up to Sacramento to see the governor so he can fix them? Or maybe it's a problem that's bigger than California. Maybe we need to get into the White House to sit down with the president. But what's the likelihood of that happening? What are the odds of any one of us standing before the U.N. or any other great political body? The chances are minimal. But you know what? We have an audience with the King of the universe any time we want it.

We already know that the governor can't really fix anything nor can the president or the U.N. But we know that God can handle everything and that nothing is too hard for Him. God can change any situation. God can change the one thing that no human government can change: the heart of a human being. And in changing the heart of one human being, He can change the course of history. That's amazing. We have access to God, and we can come to Him in the name of Jesus Christ and pour out all the problems and needs before Him, whether they are personal, national, or global.

Five times a week, I meet with a handful of men for prayer. As we pray, we try to cover the entire world nation by nation. We pray for world and religious leaders, for political and social problems, for those effected by catastrophe, and for believers in every nation. We pray for all of these different things, and we pray to the One who can do something about them. Occasionally we get reports back of how God has worked in such and such a place, and it was something about which we had specifically prayed. This privilege belongs only to the people of God. There are lots of people praying, but the only ones who have the ear of God are the children of God through faith in Jesus Christ. So, you see, we and we alone are able to do the one thing that so desperately needs to be done. Pray!

I think one of the biggest problems in the church today is the tendency to lean on man by seeking to gain political power and position. That was never God's intention for the church. How many times are we going to make this mistake before we learn? How many elections have to come and go where we have people telling us, "We've got to get the right people in office. You've got to vote for this person." Does anything ever really change? No, it all stays pretty much the same. When are we going to learn that it's through prayer? I'm not saying that we shouldn't be involved in the political process. Rather, if our hope is in a certain man or party getting into office, we're going to be repeatedly disappointed. Our hope must be in the Lord, and we must seek Him in prayer. God is able to do things we could never dream of or imagine through prayer. We often look at situations from the human standpoint that are completely impossible and think, "How could that ever be changed? How could that ever be dealt with?" But God has a way.

Think back to the mass of people that came out of Egypt, as they found themselves up against the Red Sea with mountains on both sides of them and the Egyptian army racing toward them. Do you think a single one of those persons ever thought for a moment that God would divide the Sea and send them across it in safety? I don't. In fact, I don't even think

Moses thought that. God does the unthinkable. He's able to do that. Whether it's in your own life personally, your family, your community, your church, or your country, alteration comes as we pray.

I'd like to draw your attention to one final passage in Luke. The context is the baptism of Jesus. "When all the people were baptized, it came to pass that Jesus also was baptized; and while *He prayed*, the heaven was opened. And the *Holy Spirit descended* in bodily form like a dove upon Him"[44] (emphasis mine). Notice the connection. Jesus is in prayer once again, as we've seen Him in all of these different pictures. And now as He's in prayer, what happens? The Holy Spirit descends upon Him. This is where Jesus received the baptism of the Spirit. Jesus here received the empowering to go out and to accomplish the work that the Father had sent Him to do. And this empowering came upon Him while He was in prayer.

The great need of the hour is for a fresh outpouring of the Holy Spirit. You see, when the Holy Spirit is poured out, things happen—unbelievable things, powerful things. What happens to the world at large when the Holy Spirit is poured out? Jesus said, "When the Holy Spirit comes, He will convict the world of sin."[45] We live in an exceedingly sinful world; yet many people today don't even think sin exists. People's hearts are as hard as stone. What can be done? The Holy Spirit must come. Only then will people come under conviction of sin.

What happens when the Holy Spirit is poured out upon the church? We receive power to be witnesses. And what happens when you put those two things together, sinners who realize they're sinners, Christians filled with the power of God? When these two elements come together, you have a spiritual explosion, a great awakening in the culture, a radical transformation of lives and society taking place. How does it happen? As we look at history, all of the great revivals were preceded by seasons of prayer. May God inspire us as His people to become more and more diligent and disciplined in prayer.

Prayer is the key. It always has been the key. May we rediscover today that great truth. I close with a quote on prayer from Chrysostom, a Christian leader from the second century.

> The potency of prayer hath subdued the strength of fire; it had bridled the rage of lions, hushed the anarchy to rest, extinguished wars, appeased the elements, expelled demons, burst the chains of death, expanded the gates of heaven, assuaged diseases, repelled frauds, rescued cities from

destruction, stayed the sun in its course, and arrested the progress of the thunderbolt. Prayer is an all-efficient panoply, a treasure undiminished, a mine which is never exhausted, a sky unobscured by clouds, a heaven unruffled by the storm. It is the root, the fountain, the mother of a thousand blessings.

NOTES

1   Colossians 1:18

2   1 Corinthians 15:10

3   Luke 17:10

4   1 Corinthians 4:1–2; 1 Peter 4:10

5   Acts 13:2; 15:28; 16:6

6   Acts 6:4

7   1 Corinthians 3:10–15

8   Acts 13:1

9   Ephesians 2:20

10   John 3:30

11   Matthew 5:13

12   Damian Kyle is the senior pastor of Calvary Chapel Modesto, CA. For more information or teaching archives, go to: www.ccmodesto.com.

13   2 Timothy 2:15; 4:2

14   1 Corinthians 2

15   Bil Gallatin is the founding pastor of Calvary Chapel Finger Lakes, NY. For more information or teaching archives, go to: www.ccfingerlakes.org.

16   1 Thessalonians 1:5

17   Ephesians 4:11

18   For information on Nick Long or Calvary Chapel Siegen, go to: www.calvarychapelsiegen.de. The Web site's default language is German, but English text is available.

19 For information regarding Jeff Johnson, Pancho Juarez, or Steve Mays, go to: ccdowney.com, www.cc-mtb.com, or www.ccsouthbay.org respectively.

20 2 Corinthians 1:12; 11:3

21 Acts 2:42

22 1 Samuel 9:1

23 2 Corinthians 1:12

24 Mark 14:15; Acts 1:4

25 Zechariah 4:6

26 Luke 11:9–10, 13

27 Acts 2:42

28 Ephesians 4:16

29 1 Corinthians 14:24–25

30 1 Corinthians 12:31

31 John 13:35

32 1 Timothy 1:5

33 1 Peter 1:22; 1 John 4:7–8

34 Ephesians 4:3

35 1 Peter 4:8

36 1 Peter 2:9

37 Romans 13:10

38 1 Corinthians 13:1–8, 13

39 E. M. Bounds, *Power Through Prayer*, http://www.ccel.org/ccel/bounds/power.html (accessed October 27, 2007).

40 Samuel Chadwick, *The Path of Prayer* (Sheffield, England: CLC Publications, 2000), 81.

41 Isaiah 53:2

42   Exodus 34:29–30
43   2 Corinthians 3:6–8
44   Luke 3:21–22
45   John 16:8

CONTACT INFORMATION

If you have questions or would like more information regarding Pastor Brian's ministry, please call the following numbers:

In the US:

714.979.4422

In the UK:

+44 (0)20 8466 5365

You may also go to the following Web site for information:

www.backtobasicsradio.com

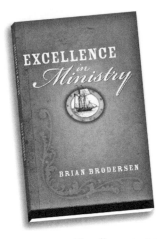

EXCELLENCE IN MINISTRY
By Brian Brodersen

978-1-59751-043-1

Excellence in Ministry is a practical guide to fruitful pastoral ministry. A companion to *Essentials in Ministry*, this new book was written for those starting out in ministry or ready to give up. Along with four insightful chapters, it contains an excellent recommended reading list as well as two teaching outlines for both a sermon and a Bible study.

Retail orders, contact:
The Word For Today
www.twft.com
800-272-9673

Wholesale orders, contact:
Calvary Distribution
www.calvaryd.org
800-444-7664